To *my very special*
MOTHER

WRITTEN BY PAM BROWN
ILLUSTRATED BY JULIETTE CLARKE
EDITED BY HELEN EXLEY

You took all the ordinary things of every
day and made me feel special. Whatever
happens in my life I know, because of you,
that I am worth something.

A HELEN EXLEY GIFTBOOK

She believes in you

Mother love is the conviction

that all her geese are swans.

Which is the only way to keep up the spirits

of kids who are convinced

that they are lame ducks.

I LOVE IT WHEN YOU ARE EXCITED

AND PLEASED BECAUSE

I'VE HAD A SUCCESS OR A STROKE OF LUCK.

AND I LOVE IT ALL THE MORE WHEN YOU STILL THINK

I'M WONDERFUL WHEN I'VE FALLEN

FLAT ON MY FACE.

*Somehow
you have made
time for me*

I don't know how you fitted me in.
But you did.
And do.

Your life is so full
– and yet I know that, always, always,
there is room for me.

Mothers applaud absolutely anything
worthy of praise.
A button done up alone. A new word.
A head-over-heels.
And the child smiles
– and soars a little higher.

A mother
doesn't care about your looks.
She thinks you are beautiful,
anyway.

*Mother love
is the most elastic
thing on earth*

Mother love
*doesn't need as much sleep
as other sorts.*

Mother love

is the most elastic thing on earth.

She is the family's pilot light.

Mother love
is more like tensile steel
than feathers.

Her love is the fuel
   that enables a normal human being
to do the impossible.

Only a mother

Only a mother
can make family
out of an assortment of
disparate individuals.

Only a mother can learn
to see through
her children's eyes.

A mother is a lady
who can do a dozen things at once

A MOTHER...

...is the lady who looks surprised
and delighted when her children bring her breakfast
at four o'clock on Mother's Day.

...has ten pairs of arms. She has to.

...is elegant with chewed rusk
in the embroidery of her evening gown.

...is the woman on the beach putting
the final touch to a sand version
of Mad King Ludwig of Bavaria's
most extravagant castle
– while her children sit throwing stones at sticks.

And she finds time to kiss
a bruised knee better

Thank you for a lifetime of caring for me

Thank you for earning the money to raise me.

Thank you for meeting me at the school gate.

Thank you for dealing with that Horrible Boy.

Thank you for putting raisins in my lunch bag.

Thank you for explaining Taking Away and Multiplying.

Thank you for making mumps not too bad at all.

Thank you for always being there when I need you.

And for Surprises.

Thank you for giving me,
your complete attention when I explained
calculus to you.

Mothers start our lives.

They cast on our existence.

They teach us plain and purl.

They give us the basic patterns.

But the good ones – the ones like you –

hand over the needles after a while,

and say:

"There's the world, love.

Choose yourself some new shades,

some new patterns.

Make yourself a life."

Good mothers give their children
paints and brushes and canvas,
     but let them paint their own picture.

Letting me be free

From the very moment I was born,

you insisted that I was myself and not an extension

of you and Dad – that I had not come into existence

simply for you to organize

or even to love.

Dear parents – thank you for giving me

the freedom to love you.

to be me

Thank you

Thank you for stocking me up with poems

and tunes to last me all my life.

Thank you for showing me

the setting sun for the first time.

And walking me in the pouring rain.

And scrunching down winter beaches.

Thank you for letting me bring home rocks

and shells and fallen branches.

Thank you for housing my frogs.

Thank you for the excitement of being alive.

For enduring...
For giving...
For loving...

Thank you for enduring the unendurable.

For making something out of nothing.

For giving when your pockets were empty.

For loving us when we were totally unlovable.

Thank you for doing the impossible

with a smile.

Mothers are the only people who
tell you the truth
when it's going to hurt.

A mother is the person you need when absolutely no one else will do.

When it's sorrow beyond keeping, phone home.

Mothers can dry your tears down a telephone.

A mother has the magic glue that sticks broken pieces together.

L̲ove is exciting. But sometimes one needs

quiet kitchen, a cup of coffee and one's mother.

Mothers have every intention of letting you go,

letting you lead your own life, never interfering.

But they just can't help phoning

to see if you have enough socks. And are eating properly.

A mother is the lady with drawers jammed with finger paintings, handmade greetings cards, plasticine cats, certificates and medals. And who could not be persuaded to part with one of them.

I am proud of you

Take in the laundry. Collect the mended shoes.

Reading tests and driving tests and interviews.

Telephone and train times. P.T.A.

Cheese and crackers and pet rabbit hay.

Computers and portfolios, manuscripts and mice.

E-mail and long-grained rice.

Measle spots and mergers, the ballet school display.

I am proud
of what you do.
I love you
for what you are.

When I was small
          and afraid

When I was very small and afraid,
you used to put on the light and show me
all the familiar objects in my room
– then flick it off and sit with me in the darkness
until I was quite certain the shapes were constant.

You would always sneak a crack of light
into the gloom – just enough to let me see that
nothing stalked my bed.

In a way it's still the same.
My anxieties are greater now, and my world less certain
– but you let a little light into it, so I can see my problems
for what they are.
Things I can deal with – not run from.

MEMORIES OF CHILDHOOD

I remember the run home from school,
black-stockinged, satchel swinging, the drab day behind me,
toast and currant cake ahead.
I remember the smell of home
– the smell all children hold in their noses,
the way puppy dogs do.

I remember you in the kitchen,
apron-wrapped and waiting for my news.

And now here we are, sitting in a
coffee shop, our carrier bags safely against our ankles,
exchanging the news of the week.

The years have changed us, brought us closer.
Mother and child – friends for life.

If I ever really need my mother...

I know if I turned up on the doorstep

in the middle of the night, soaked through,

with all my bags and speechless with tears you'd just say,

"Oh, love. Take off all your clothes.

Put on my big woolly dressing gown."

Let's hope it will never come to that.

But it's nice to know.

Thank you for being there come fire,

flood or penury.

Thank you for being ready

to lend anything,

give anything that will help us

deal with whatever life brings.

Mothers are an interlocking chain that holds the world together.

MOTHERS

You know exactly what life is all about.
Not Art. Not Literature.
Not Science. All interesting stuff. Worth doing.
But basically, basically, it's about children,
about people. You mothers should be the politicians.

ACROSS THE WORLD

Mothers are strange creatures.

It's true.

Even when their kids are middle-aged

they worry about their underwear. And socks.

And summer colds.

They worry when the roads are icy.

Or when there's an epidemic.

And mothers worry about childish weaknesses

long outgrown.

They need to keep in touch.

They phone at inconvenient moments.

They smile bright crocodile smiles

at friends of whom they don't approve.

They refuse to give up on you – no matter what!

LETTING GO

Your hands held mine until I could walk alone.
You taught me freedom
– and when the time had come you let me go.

Thank you for being interested
– but never prying.
For being loving – but never drowning me in love.
For building me a nest – but letting me fly free.

Thanks for opening all those doors for me
– but never shoving me through them.

A life filled with

If a thing was worth seeing,

or hearing or smelling or touching or testing

– you would get me there

– come hell or high water, come mud,

snow, rain or lack of cash in hand.

Thank you for a life filled with memories

to see me through.

memories

One part of a mother's mind
is constantly upon her children, however adult,
however sophisticated they may have become.
She studies, calculates, arranges,
runs enterprises, writes books, sees clients,
concludes experiments,
deals with patients, gives sound professional advice.
But, always, a little section of her brain is reserved
for family matters and at every pause
in the pressures of the day
will turn to such concerns as slipped discs,
mortgages, pregnancies
– and the recipe for carrot cake she promised.

Love –

constant love

She is someone who has learned to love
and can never after get out of the habit.

STANDING

Thanks for not giving up on me
when I'd been particularly awful. You were
the only one who didn't.

You took all the ordinary things of every day
and made me feel special.

Whatever happens in my life I know, because of you,

that I am worth something.

Always there

Thank you for always being there.
Not intrusively. Not demandingly.
There.
Available at all hours for advice on coughs,
spelling, good books, stains, Mozart,
friends' presents, using libraries, crossword clues.
Ready to come if needed. At once.
Shoulder to cry on.
Someone to tell the news.
Someone to laugh at the Funny.
Someone with an inexhaustible supply of love.
Whatever I've done.
Always.